Archetypal Light

Western Literature Series

University of Nevada Press ▲▲ Reno & Las Vegas

Archetypal Light

Elizabeth Dodd

P O E M S

WESTERN LITERATURE SERIES

University of Nevada Press, Reno, Nevada 89557 USA

Copyright © 2001 by Elizabeth Dodd

All rights reserved

Manufactured in the United States of America

Library of Congress Cataloging-in-Publication Data

Dodd, Elizabeth Caroline, 1962–

Archetypal light : poems / Elizabeth Dodd.

p. cm. — (Western literature series)

ISBN 0-87417-365-5 (alk. paper)

1. West (U.S.)—Poetry. 2. Nature—Poetry. I. Title.

II. Series.

PS3554.03177 A89   2001

811'.54—dc21   00-011121

The paper used in this book meets the requirements
of American National Standard for Information
Sciences—Permanence of Paper for Printed Library
Materials, ANSI Z39.48-1984. Binding materials were
selected for strength and durability.

FIRST PRINTING

10 09 08 07 06 05 04 03 02 01

5 4 3 2 1

Anniversary

This morning, walking, I passed fountains
of spirea, light May breeze
shaking the languorous arms of white
flowers, sky bright as your eyes
the day we looked — across the distance
of possibility — at each other, and chose
this life we're living, dancing
together as the whole bush breathes and blossoms.

Yesterday, under the continual murmur of cottonwoods,
we found a warbling vireo. You saw it first,
but when it sang, I knew that language, from my childhood:
riparian celebration, woodland songburst.
I've heard that music all my life, under oak and beech tree;
yet like so many things we find to share, you give it to me.

Contents

Acknowledgments

Grateful acknowledgment is made to the editors of the following journals, where versions of these poems first appeared:

"The Work" and "Jim Bachae's New Hip" (1998) in *Seneca Review;* "Virginia Rail" (1998) and "Variations on the Horizontal" (1998) in *Ascent;* "Prairie Hills in Snow" (1998) in *Flint Hills Review;* "Northwest Passage" (1998) in *Gulf Coast;* "Archetypal Light," "The Route," "Corduroy Road," "Parietal" (1998) in *Proteus: A Journal of Ideas;* "The Door" (1997) in *Crab Orchard Review;* "The Blue of the Mussel Shell" (1997) in *Crazyhorse;* "Lake Florissant" (1997) in *High Plains Literary Review;* "North" (1997) in *Tar River Poetry;* "American Dipper" (1996) in *CutBank;* "Southerly" (1995) in *Tar River Poetry;* "Taphonomy" (1995) in *Chariton Review;* "Bicycling in the Great Salt Marsh" (1995) in *Midwest Quarterly;* "Blackjack" (1995) in *Cimarron Review;* "At Scott's Bluff, Nebraska" (1994) in *The Virginia Quarterly Review;* "The Piebald Robin" (part 2 of "The Hudson River School") (1994) in *West Branch;* "The Hudson River School" (part 1) and "The Cave" (1994) in *Poet and Critic.*

The author also wishes to thank the Kansas Arts Commission for fellowship support, and Kansas State University for research grant support. Thanks are due as well to Jerry Dees, Roger Mitchell, Kathrine Walker Schlageck, Bill North, and the United States Forest Service.

The Cave

Sightless, shadowless,
the toothless blindcat cruises
fossil waters, dark karsts far
below the surface of this
world. Pink, translucent,
beautiful (if anyone were looking),
the blindcat grazes microbial
sludge, following some hidden ledge
or cavern floor, eating, breeding,

removed from the rhythms of daybreak,
sunset, weather. The blindcat lives
the continual present, the tactile—the gentle
wash of water on whisker, the propulsion of self
through location (not distance).
In this continued seclusion, through millennia,
the succession of their lives and bodies proves
the sublime. And if the blindcat,

rising one day through limestone and artesian
water, entered the dazzling brilliance
of sunlight, should she surface
in some Texas farmer's well,
some utility pumping station
(near San Marcos or Austin), wouldn't perhaps
the blindcat ponder for a moment (if she could)
the meaning of the real, of virtue,
and come to recognize in the dark, calm waters
of her home, this truth: *so much was she loved.*

Variations on the Horizontal

I. EQUINOX
Cormorants crossing   the air
above water,   harriers gliding,
riding the updrafts—

these movements trace the ultimate
body,
      the disappearing line

of sight.   I lie
in dry grass and cattail,

just under the wind.

In the day's last
lucent hours,   two tall white forms

leap,   lift,

                    spread wings

to reach toward each
horizon, then spiral slowly
down where everything
meets: mudflat,
                    salt marsh,
sky glint, whooping
crane,
            the quick
confluence of edges.

II. EMERGENCE
In the first world, nothing
had spoken. Therefore, distances

did not exist. The sky and water were
one skin, one shadow, curled fingertips
within the bone.

     Desire was the first
to peel away. He wished for *something*
when there was only *am*—he wished

until the tiny clots of soil and dust
began to settle out, began
their paradigm of shells.

So Grief was next. She grew a body,
sedimentary, then ascended
        to the opening air.

When she longed to sing,
spilled moonlight rippled, pooled,
until there was a moon to travel
the mathematic trails of space.

Then there were people,
cast shadows lapping at their feet.

They named themselves—Cottonwood,
Oak—and left for the illuminated
plains.

That's when Fear arrived.
She might have been
nothing, the simple
pull of cloud
                    to water,
lake to cloud,
the rasp of dry leaves underfoot.

She might—

but lifting from the level ground,
the charred, dark statues gaze.

III. CLOVIS POINT WITH MASTODON
Already the world
was changing, the plain
irrupting scars
of stone, smoke,
                    cinders drifting

like the snows the people
tried to leave behind by walking
always south.
                    Mountains rose
from the level stretch of land;
ignited by the liquid
rock, grassfires grazed
the near horizon.

                    Already they knew
to turn, move north again to the next
high mesa. Already,
the plain was littered with lava,

misshapen forms like massive
animals brought down
in the prayerful technic
of the hunt, long
before the horse
returned, even in dreams,
before the smaller bison fell
to propulsive, sudden tumors,
lead within the breast.

IV. SAVANNA
Like melody caught in the mind's
fond ear, the grasslands sang
their systemic refrain, eighty million
years
        of ripening, rhizomes, runners

tunneling under the prevailing plains.

Prairie, pampa, steppe, veld,
all echoes of Africa, legacies
of light.

        The quiet dialogue
of range and cover—
                oak openings, prairie
peninsulas, seeds and mast
rustling when wind lifts;
hair raising along the naked neck.

      The Savannah Sparrow, when flushed,
flies a short distance, quickly
dropping back down out of sight.

By nightfall, fire lined
the far horizon, the height of grass reduced
to ash.
                In wind, the flames raced
sideways.

And I stood up.

In the Dream I Am

I. MUSEUM PIECE

Frémont figurines lie in
    orderly rows, limbs and torsos
        fused in the indistinct

articulation of their bodies.
    But the faces—
        "shuttered eyes," the plaque describes.

Vacant sockets
    gaze through
        thin palings of clay.

Think of Emily Dickinson,
    eyes locked with God's,
        measuring deserts in his clemency.

II. AFTER THE ICE STORM

For days the landscape
glittered, terrible clarity
coating each tree limb,
each shrub.

The pines were marbled,
fingers no one could touch.

Last night, all night
ice fell from the house,
the trees, loosened

by yesterday's sun
and the wind's late return.

I woke to the atonal
music of change, tiny crashes
and thuds, the bodies
casting off stasis.

III. IN THE DREAM I AM
                        at the edge
of a river, squatting amid summer's
thick bracken and sumac.

I have been counseled
to dig, so I'm lifting up
fistfuls of loose dirt, weeping,
uncovering bones.

They rise slowly,
like half-waterlogged wood.

Yes, says the voice,
very good, as I hold a perfect
tibula, smooth as the dark
current's surface.

Later, I will try to tell
of the masks I saw, the faces dressed
in pigment and bone. Imagine
a skull as pliant
as pie dough, smoothed
over the ruthless planes of the face.

We can't get away, we can't
even find each other in the dark.

Someone is turning, slowly, to look.

Taphonomy

Before us lies the body   what's left
of body   bones their patterns
on the patterned dirt   a tuft of fur
the agile cast
of grass shadows

Corpus corporeal corpse the course
of flesh unwinding from its frame
unwinding

Caught in the passion
of attention we note
the jawbone dragged perhaps
by coyotes   the soil
sifting into space   the mind
once filled   we follow
weather's slow narrative
we study the body
successions of insects
economies of rot

We squat in this century's
sunlight   dust crusting already our boots
our hands the backs of our necks as
understanding accretes its hard
mineral weight   thoughts caught
in each layered image this
death this moment this

Lake Florissant

. . . twenty-four extinct species of beech tree . . .

Like words in a language
I almost remember,
these shale leaves, labeled, arranged
behind glass and the glare
of fluorescent tubes, register

somewhere in animal memory.
Sunlight sifting the canopy
of hardwoods, diffuse inflections
dependent on weather, soil,
the relative conjunctive sea.

In October, a fallen beech leaf seems
the fossil imprint of itself, the dative
case, deciduous. Bones from the early
Cenozoic: Oreodont, Mesohippus
prefigure the roots or broken limbs

as the tree branches outward. Coshow, Coçeau—
my mother's people said their narrow feet
were the Indian past behind them,
French-Canadian, forgotten.
High, youthful cheekbones and a gilt-

edged frame, my aunt and mother watch me,
mutely black-and-white. Beech leaves settled
on ash-stricken waters. Mesohippus died
or changed, equine expansion leading into
disappearance. When finally the horse

returned, traveling northward
from the Spanish into the lives
of Great Plains peoples,
what could the herds remember,
or imagine?

At Scott's Bluff, Nebraska,

                                      wind
is the language of this morning,
as I'm climbing
Me-a-pa-te, "hill that is hard
to go around," high above
surrounding grasslands, badlands.
White-throated swallows in midmorning heat
loop and chitter over rock face or juniper,
my feet pausing
at each edge of bluff, enough
to almost call me either
upwards in ecstatic flight
or down in death. My breath is lost
between the points of Saddle Rock;
I'm squinting into
wingbeat of magpie,
sussurant grass stem, timeless
sunlight, sky—

Imagine the earth as self-
elegy, memory articulated
into headland, stone,
volcanic ash and harder caprock, life
translated slowly into layers.
White stone against bright sky, I
can't hear the words not spoken, only know
this is memory, this
could be grief.

Imagining the Journey West

Somewhere outside Topeka, in sod walls
and wind, incessant, a woman caught
in the preponderant present
could lose everything she had been, once.

Prairie fire washes the surface, erasing
the image, like memory emptied, bison bones
whitening in the tallgrass
to the blank page's stark glare.

One western morning, in front of the house,
I face eastward, envision leaving
Ohio, by wagon or buckboard,
before trillium's articulate

springtime arrival, before
the garrulous patter of raindrops on mayapples,
slant light on dogwood,
and leaving my father,

his hand holding forever its two-syllable gesture,
fare-well, believing, in such continental distance,
I would always carry that moment,
my last connection to the voice that named me.

Virginia Rail

common but secretive, the only small North American rail with a long bill

The eye lifts to the shimmer
of sky and water,
breeze-riffled reeds where the bird

is just slipping from sight,
bill first and rounded body after;
this bird I've waited for—

streaked olive back, rusty breast—
loving the name, *Virginia Rail,*
which gives me back my childhood.

In Mr. Kestler's music class,
one Friday a month, in East Elementary's
dusty basement music room,

we danced. Over scratchy recordings
of fiddle and banjo, Mr. Kestler's voice
described a world we'd live in

for an hour, awkward bodies practicing
the square dance, that social geometry
of partners, corners, allegoric orders

touching, briefly, hands.
Or my favorite, the Virginia reel's
democratic pattern where

we all presided, each in sequence,
as head couple, arms lifted in the arch
a nation, headed westward, might pass through.

And what I assume, you shall assume.
In Quivira, Kansas, wetland named
when Coronado camped here,

seeking the elusive
city of gold,
where history seems glazed

and glimmering in late
September light, while the rail enters
the standing reeds, I'm left

beside the salt marsh squinting, trying to see.

The Door

On display at the Trading Post Museum is the door to John Brown's fort, built near the town of Trading Post, Kansas, after the Marais des Cygnes Massacre, a raid on Free State settlers led by Georgian Charles Hamelton, in May 1858. Earlier, John Brown had led a similar strike: in May 1856, Brown and others (including John Brown Jr. who had come by steamboat and wagon to homestead in the area with his wife, Wealthy) raided the cabins of two pro-slavery families, killing five men. Minnie Cameron gave the door to Vina Conoway (later Priestley) as payment for domestic work.

I. WEALTHY HOTCHKISS BROWN

Well, you know doors are always opening
or closing. When you haven't got one, then
you come to know how fine a door can be.
That first year in Kansas, Jason and John Jr.
rode each day or so to Lawrence, never
troubling to start a house. We camped
all summer, huddled under canvas flaps—
smoke always in my eyes, no matter how
I squinted, where I sat, I couldn't see
to cook, or where our lives might lead to.
Winter hit early, October stunned
beneath a sky so bruised with clouds the wind
could never clear away one front of darkness
for another. That's when their father came,
The Cause so livid in him that he never
felt the cold. That's when we got three walls,
a roof, but even if I'd had a door to bolt
it couldn't have saved us from the grief we followed.
Yes, we stalked our troubles, chased them clear
across this troubled land. Traveling west
I watched the steamboat's paddlewheel turn—
such power and a grace so grim. By day

the sun might glitter on the dripping water
but in the dark the current always slipped
beneath us, moving east while we went west.
What we think is loveliness or truth
grinds us toward some horror or another.
How could I know The Cause would come to murder,
John Brown pulling neighbors from their homes
to slit their throats and call it justice? And then
my husband closed a portion of his heart.
We'd lie awake at night, not talking,
and I knew he felt so lonely in that world
that was our lives, a darkened room where we
stood by the threshold, seeing far too much
but also not enough to know what we should do.

II. VINA CONOWAY PRIESTLEY
Sometimes I felt that land was haunted, when
I'd walk right by the draw where all those men
were shot. We grew up with the story,
though it happened forty years before:
that Georgia devil, Charles Hamelton,
rode in one afternoon and rounded up
Free Staters, pulled them from their fields, from
the very saddles, sometimes, they were sitting in—
and then he lined them up and fired.
Four decades later, Minnie Cameron
could fill the house with stories, those men
almost in the room with us. I loved
to hear her voice go soft and pause,
midsentence, when she felt her baby move.
Those months I helped her with her laying-in,
I cleaned and cooked and coaxed her appetite

with porridge in a pretty china bowl.
I think that year that I was happy.
Later, for a keepsake, Minnie gave me
John Brown's door, saved from his fort—somehow
her Daddy'd kept it all those years, although
they'd long since torn the fort down, plowed the land,
and now I don't recall just where it stood.
It seems we have so little left to touch
or tie us to our past. But I remember
sunny days I'd bring the wash and find
a flock of flycatchers perched on the line.
They'd lift off in a flash of sudden
color, hover for a moment overhead,
and I'd stand still enough I'd think God would
reveal something, time or Providence
resolve itself across the fields
like brilliant planks of sunlight through
the broken summer storms. Sometimes,
wind twisting laundry in my hands,
I'd think I sensed the vanished dead.
Have you ever watched the grasses flash
in sudden shadow when wind moves them
like an unseen hand, or like the ghosts
of slaves obscured from view? Such changes coming
we can't see, and can't yet understand.

Prairie Hills in Snow

I. PSYCHE

In wind, the hills ripple
into disappearing
distance. And the white drifts—
for days, no one has spoken.

Above the snow, broken
stalks dangle, occasional
gestures of the dead.

Everything has gone under
the surface.

II. SCAR

When the dog broke through
and floundered in near-freezing
water, the man couldn't stop
himself, leaped in
and threw her clear, so she stood
whining, shivering, watching

while he couldn't lift himself free.
She watched while he slowly
moved toward shore,
slamming both fists
to break the lake ice,
moving into the pathway he carved
with his arms: fist, move, fist, move.

They rode home together
in the heated truck. Nightfall,
no stars, the open
water already was closing,
growing an imperfect
but serviceable skin.

III. BURIAL
Along the river trail
a few more trees are down,
cottonwoods four feet across.
Last year's flood, an ice storm—

their stopped carcasses
block the path.

Downstream, the swollen river
heaped the fields
with sand.
    Once, perhaps weary of land,
ancestral whales walked back
to the waters, imagining
a different life.

I stand in the wind.

Loose snow skitters
in the raw air.

North

In mid-November, 18 degrees, cold air
astounds, astringent in the lungs.

Last night I listened to the high,
southward travel of geese.
Occluded moon, few
stars, the dark surroundings centered
all attention
                on the aural, goose cries
articulating—what? Trajectory? Self?
The brief pandemic
yes exhaled among the world's
occasioned bodies?

                When Albert Bierstadt painted
Near North Conway, everything he saw
was static presence: foregrounded rocks, a wall
of pines, then meadow under
heavy clouds, surrounding mountains,
and only a dim,
                distant glimmer
shining from the farthest lake.

Sometimes the spirit
loses touch with matter.
Ice tumbles from a cliff face
and a woman leaps aside
or doesn't, body rooted
in despair, or not.

This morning dawn recalls
the river glazing its own
frozen banks, the young hardwoods,
the fallen depth of leaves.

The tent is sheathed
inside with ice,
                  the material
attendance of our breaths.

The Hudson River School

I.

Above drift classic, backlit clouds, connections
to the beautiful and true. In day's last
light, I'm leaning in my lawn chair,
headphones centering their music

where mind meets body, that spot
Descartes described three centuries before
I bought this compact disc, this six-pack.

Hackberry leaves purl and ripple
in the evening breeze's shiver,
silvering in the last angled
rays of daylight.

The tree trunks are green with sudden lichen;
all day the grass
alchemized air and light into
matter.
            Almost hidden, thumb-high,
tiny cedars breathe earth into air,
rootlets soaking up life from the poachy ground.

A lip of light glints along the birdbath;
you could almost touch the image,
or the thing itself.

I click off the music, listen
to a robin's final call before
she drinks and leaves for the darker pines.

II.

Suddenly, white
tail feathers, beige-and-white
patches on the back and head; yet red-
breasted, a frosted robin,

body oddly
allegorical, tiny oracle,
a mind of winter; no—

a bird pulling September
worms from the lawn.
I watch the piebald detail
of his body, foregrounded
in this backyard prospect:

hackberry trees, a stand
of cedars by the cedar fence,
the woodpile, and,

unlike so many tiny paintstrokes
of suggested birds, almost
unnoticed in the panorama,

these presences, truth
so often various,
whether one watches, or not.

Depth Image

—after Clarence Morgan

As the human
eye desires   light
and movement,   seeks out

an interior
          elegance, circumstance,
edges of contact,
hesitation

at the clearing's
brink,   attention sinking
through the textured

presences   ventricles
cerulescent in the self,
the necessary ruminous

accretion,   drift,
molecular shifting

as the warm hand   lifts, the wind
continues, ice closes
the open   waters,

discovers beloved structures,
layered,
     latent,   this lake's
floating trellis.

Within the Bright Potential

Was somebody asking to see the soul?

In Rockwell Kent's *Alaska,*
it is clear the world
is light, the liquid translucent
forms of mountains,
icebergs rising
                    from pellucid waters,

then the only
slightly lighter sky. And I

can just recall acute
Canadian summer sunlight,
lake surface glinting

like my mother's beaded sweater
while my father held me up
to see.

                    Last night dreams took me
to a mountain river,
stone-dark waters,
unseen streambed inaccessible
as our first, wordless
thoughts.
                    I stood, or dreamed
I stood among the mosses'
primeval cities,
                    singular

beneath the evergreens
and mist.

        Within the river
current's ancient chaos,
detaching from a granite
boulder, half-submerged,

a plumed bird
              lifted, shook
the lichens from its eyes
and turned to see me,
rock softening to feathers,

flesh, the graceful phenomenal
presence paint
           approximates, the
sacred hesitation
of these words across the page,
dark marks within
the circumambient bright potential.

As It Happens This Morning,

this mountain lake gives everything back,
perfecting the thought
of reflection: ragged evergreens reach
in each of their two great directions;
slanted granite's tilt skyward
angles, acute with the water's clear
image of uplift. I listen—no wind.

This alpine light blooms mineral
glints in the talus slope,
sulphur flower's yellow puffs.
Facing the day's continuing
motion, I stoop by a blackened circle
of stones, dry twigs in hand
for another small, essential fire.

Archetypal Light

Almost silent, the canoe
slips
    into bayou
backwater, past

lilypads, algae,
swaying webs of moss,

the dark still repetition,
variation,

        the trees the bank the
day's clear skies our arms

lifting in each
slow stroke.

Ancient patience,
an alligator hangs
in the bald cypress shadows.

Cloud,
    light,
shade from the near tree meets
my body's skin.

Light, cloud,
      light—

a red-eared slider suns
on a log.

No current, so we
are the current.

This is the journey, again
the journey, we are

crossing the water
we follow the channel

the sun crosses the far
pool, the blue
lake's surface shudders under

our motion, darkens,
returns its bright still composition.

An arm of moss touches
my hair, my face,
as I face forward.

Southerly

Wind-driven, loose grass and dried bracken
rush past.
          Turning, banking, my hair,
the hawk's wing, hanging—

Each second
breathes the balance, essence
or accident caught
in the updraft, rising
in the throat.

Language is an organ
of the mind, says Chomsky.

Rose verbena has suddenly
colored the hillsides.
Compass plants scratch
stiff leaves along the ground.

The harrier drops
past the lip of the hill. The sun climbs,
as we say,
                though it doesn't,
but still I am standing
in springtime,
                the deep structure
of seasons, warming
to all that I know
or don't,

wondering whether
the hawk will come back,

giving myself to this hovering
and open sky, pause
in the sentence,
turn in the line.

Bicycling in the Great Salt Marsh

On the packed sand road my tires
merely whisper; still
I scare up teal,
ruddy ducks, white-faced ibis,
scuttling flocks of coots.

They lift and settle farther out.

Yet past the road's south curve,
the reeds are filled
with egrets, slender necks, wings
outstretched or bent, graceful
bodies in the cattails. Thousands—
cattle egrets, snowy, great, all
staying in the swaying marsh
while I ride past.

Everyone I love
is elsewhere,
                    yet this morning distance
appears illusory, like the course of Zeno's arrow
that can always be divided
into *here,* then *here,* so many points
of stasis. Pausing I stand

among a cloud of blackbirds moving
as one body, the way a school of fish
will travel or define the larger whole.
Wind and sun touch the water,
touch my skin. Nothing has moved.

Form and Theory

I. IMMANENCE

The light dust
breath
the light, crusting
on the body

Papillary grasses,
near wind in the pinyons

The light strikes
the cliff wall, scattered
sand

II. GEORGIA O'KEEFFE

"I just tried to paint what I saw"

Because of the lovely curve
of the pelvis,
because of the beautiful
angle of hill against
sky, because of the joy
and the cast shadow's hue.
Because the abstraction
inheres in the object.
Because of the open
door in the wall.

III. FUMAROLE CONES

A remembered hiss
of ash caught

in steam's quick
flash.

Open holes in the stone,
the archaic helix
of ascension.

Red rock.
Two miles down the trail—
white.

Buttresses
slowing erosion's old
grind against the cliffs.

In the day's last sun,
they become
birdsong. In the gray dawn,
they are mammoth
bones.

Overcast sky, midnight,
wind flutes through
the darkened canyon.

Catastrophism

When I follow the line
of your arm, pointing,
I can't see how
I missed it, the cleft in the rock
or the rock wren
momentarily still
against rock face and sagebrush.

Look, and your eyes find
the columnar shape
of the raven, silent, profiled,
one eye wide and stony, focusing
outward.

        Palouse Falls plummets
two hundred feet from that jagged,
jointed body of basalt.

Exhale—
a long, shivering breath, arhythmic—

In the twentieth century's spasmodic
second decade, Eugene C. Bretz staggered over
the still-young "channeled scablands,"
—older also than the roots
of the language he wrote in—
telling himself the probable:

upheavals, ancient Lake Missoula flooding
westward, until even rivers remember.

Because existence is
sequential crisis, the sharp articulation
of our keenest days. This poem holds
cascading anguish at a parent's death;

the swift, unlooked-for
passion when lives pool, lovely,
although mutable.

Triptych: Jump Studies

I. CATARACT

He hangs, toe-
holds and hands almost
horizontal, head
slightly lower than his hips.

He slips,
leaps or drops then
dances,
        briefly, seeking

                balance.

My brother studies the cliff
for the possible
climb; I'm basking, watching
how, just now,
        the mountain pool

composes all
the visible into this
convergent form.

Pale slant
of my legs; the angle
trees tumbled
        when they fell,
broke
against edged rock;

              shadow-slant
of standing trunks;
sunlight tracing illusory
galaxy-pathways through
the forest's height.

The waterfall
never falters, arcing
white droplets graceful
in the physics of the plunge.

Wind, or water-
roar, or blood beat
pulses in my ears.

If any of us shouted,
none would hear.

II. DIVIDE
The rock stops, drops
near-vertical, there
where two steps could reach.

I'm wedged against
the cliff, just inches
from the mountain-

goat who wishes
—urgent, hesitant—
to pass by.

I look away,
press hands
to the lichen-painted

face of stone, Precambrian
microbial pictographs
imagined and

while this human
thought turns back
and down, the young

goat leaps, moves
on. Eyes closed,
I try to hold

the singular,
slight drumming
of his stride.

III. KILL SITE
Open grass chitter
dickcissel rock
wren the trail bends
rises tracing the
ancient way
down to water

reversing the journey
we climb into mid–
summer's high
daylight bright
heat lifting already
the raptors
spirals air sketches

we move into the near
wind the headland

invites attention
high distant mountain-
chain snow cloaks blue
prospects the river

we scatter grasshoppers
our walking discovers
pale flakings of bone
a hawk feather lost
from the dry sky bone
chips at the cliff's
blind high plummet

we don't talk stop
breathe imagine back.

The Labrador Duck

(extinct since 1878)

1. BEACON

Out of sight, just past
the trail's bend,
a child is asking, *Daddy,
is this an island?*

Almost invisible in mist,
the lighthouse gestures
only upwards, unilluminated—
vacant windows, clapboard roof,
a Bay of Fundy relic.

Someone summons: *Time to go.*

Fog shrouds the shore,
the high-tide stretch of wet
stones, smooth with repetition,
each wave's lift and hurl and drop.

2. DIORAMA

In the blue light of depicted
winter, Long Island Sound
is snow, ocean, and Labrador
Ducks, floating close
to the factitious shore.

Schoolchildren hurry past,
headed for the sauropods.

In those distorted voices,
the silent specimens
are bright-eyed, diving
or startled almost into flight.

When I turn back,
one lifted wing seems poised
against me, an arm before the face.

3. MEMENTO
I linger at the water's edge.
Each rock against my palm is time
as matter, the geologic pressed
into the historic, the fingers'
living curl and crest.

Corduroy Road

Crossing the high
wet slope, ascending
through second-growth evergreen,
aspen, we pass abandoned
machinery, colossal rusted
cables, gears, years
of exposure velveting
the iron exterior.

Like a single idea given
efficient form, the equipment
seems paused in midsentence,
or rather waiting, after
double click on "placer gold,"
for text to appear.

On the map, tiny icons—
picks and axes—mark mines,
auxiliaries of empire left
along the Crooked River and
the River Road, the 19th-century
port of entry to the present site.

Gospel-Hump: a wilderness
of pack trails, bear grass,
black bear but no grizzly,
imported chukar, maturing timber,

cougar, and the rocks my brother
scrambles for a higher view.

This afternoon we don't discover
Crystal Lake, turn back
the way we came. Creek crossings,
rock-clotted meadow, then the miners' road,
logs slowly rotting, parallel, the historic
textured surface that we follow down.

The Route

". . . we study how to deserve
what has already been given us."
—WILLIAM STAFFORD

I. PIONEER MOUNTAINS, MID-JULY

I rest against dull stone
and lichen, count drifting cirrus wisps
until the water boils.

Buckwheat noodles, powdered broth,
canned chicken and the dandelion leaves
hand-gathered on the trail.

Halfway to the headwaters
of Osborne Creek, we eat on a high
subalpine point among
these actualities: aspen
scattered through the pine-
wrapped slopes; far distant granite
peaks in snow; invisible, our meadow
cabin and its barrel stove.

Two miles back, we passed
burnt fir and spruce trees, wreckage
trenched into the mountain dirt:
the littered crash site where, last winter,
a single-engine plane went down.
I imagine traveling
against the inchoate face
of storm, against chaotic
translation of one
into another, old meteor

dross turned water droplets,
swirling, static
just before he hit—

Ahead, we hope
to find a rumored stand
of seven-hundred-year-old trees,
rare alpine larch. Quick northern
summer and long days
of light, I'm living fully
in the body, hungry
for each elevated apperception, for
each evening fire, each
day's book and map and boot.

II. DAYBOOK—SCATTERED NOTES

In winter, a handful of dried stinging nettles added to boil-
ing soup broth will reconstitute bright green and delicious,
much like fresh nettle plants in spring. Crumbled leaves are
especially good in cream of potato soup or vegetable stew.

Dandelion leaves are good added to soups, stews, scrambled
eggs, omelets, and quiche. Tender young leaves need not be
cooked and make a good addition to tossed salad. . . . To
avoid bitterness, dandelion leaves are best if picked before
the heat of the day and from plants that have not yet pro-
duced flowers that season. . . . Some settlers, once they real-
ized the Great Plains were devoid of dandelions, wrote
back to Europe for seeds and carefully planted dandelions
in their yards and gardens.

—Kay Young, *Wild Seasons: Gathering and*
Cooking Wild Plants of the Great Plains

Meriwether Lewis to William Irvin, April 15, 1803: Portable Soup, in my opinion, forms the most essential articles in the preparation, and fearing that it cannot be procured readily in such quantity as is requisite, I take the liberty to request that you will procure some 200 pounds of it for me. . . . I have supposed that the soup would cost about one dollar pr pound; should it, however, come much higher then quantity must be limited by the sum of $250 as more cannot be expended.

Flowers: Fool Hen Cabin
cinquefoil
    snow lily
        globe flower

silvery lupine
    subalpine blue violet
        pink monkeyflower

sulphur flower
    salsify
        scarlet paintbrush

pearly everlasting
    greenleaf chiming bell
        marsh marigold

stonecrop
    shooting star

(Note: near cabin, *white* shooting star—one plant, three blossoms in a field of pink and purple blooms.)
(Note also: dandelions!)

III. WHEN SERGEANT FLOYD TOOK SICK,
("cramp cholic" / burst appendix?)
he was (though no one knew this, yet)
the only member of the Corps to die
along the route.
                          Captain Lewis
had just turned thirty. Private Reed,
deserter, was court-martialed on the banks
of the Missouri, Oto chiefs attending,
Clark recorded, asking "Pardin for this man."

Private Shannon soon would disappear,
spend sixteen days in chase
of his companions, thinking
he was left behind until, at last,
the Corps caught up and found him
starving, gaunt, propped up along
the water's edge and waiting.
He was nineteen.
                          In 1833, Maximilian, Prince of Weid,
would pass Floyd's grave and write, "a short
stick marks the grave where he is laid
and has often been renewed by travellers
when the fires in the prairie have distroyed it."

IV. CAMAS
Mid-November, 1805, Clark notes the vote
on where to situate
Fort Clatsop: York (a slave),
Sacagawea (nicknamed Janey—
woman, captive, child bride),
each says which Pacific
shore should be preferred.

They're making ready
for the winter, wet
along the northwest coast.

They'll shoot lean, stringy elk and little else.

Sacagawea knows the roots
to keep the Corps from starving;
Clark remarks, in understated ink,
"Janey in favour of a place
where there is plenty of Potas."

(Yet York and Janey, members
of the Corps, won't vote within
the body politic, their suffrage
suffered only like two bright
erratics, exotic stones transported
in the glacial past.)

Later, early summer
as the Corps moves east, it's Lewis
who describes the camas (quamash) flowering:
"from the colour of its bloom
at a short distance it resembles
lakes of fine clear water, so complete
is this deseption that on first sight
I could have swourn it was water."

V. GLACIAL MILL
In Philadelphia and elsewhere, Lewis
shopped for the almost
unimaginable, designing
folding boats that wouldn't

float, procuring cannisters
for powder, kettles, blue glass beads

to trade along the river
bluffs and tributaries, globes of
sky and color, power
in the captains' hands,
advancing.

Blue turquoise water
leaves a glacier,
shivers down the
metamorphic slope
of uplift, grinding rock powder
from the Lewis range, Precambrian,
the river rasping
while the glaciers shrink.

At Big Two Medicine Lake,
almost a mile of Pleistocene ice
preceded Lewis, Clark,
these three mergansers pausing
in the turquoise cove.
The lake suspends
bright glacial flour.
We lift our paddles,
point toward shore.

VI. THIRD WEEK OF SEPTEMBER, WIND
out of the southwest, the wash
all dries by mid-day.

Walking to the office, the body feels
at ease, unweighted briefly in this
wind that lifts. Even the hackberries
sound like cottonwoods. Ninety-seven, ninety-eight,
the mercury clings to summer, but
new walnut hulls begin
to blacken on the blacktop.

Blackjack

When my great-great-
grandfather Ace Gutowsky
followed his doodlebug, lucked his way
into oil at last, a genuine
gusher, he must have felt fate
riding his body like a full hip flask,
warming to his touch like a silver
dollar heavy in his palm.
Luck must have stuck
by him, clear from Kiev, into
Oklahoma and the flat
expanse of shortgrass prairie, past
the dustbowl and the almost-
over war. In 1944,
the man leans into the photograph, counting
on confidence to see us all through.

My aunt keeps the copy
of *Time* magazine, its time-
darkened dream of peacetime kitchens, toasters,
advertising the almost-tomorrow, and her great-
grandfather's story reading
American dreaming, eyes locked
to the camera, not focusing beyond
the page in hand.

I'm driving north on Highway 10,
through hills along the Illinois River,

past towns where all the hands
have folded. This landscape alternates
patches of pasture and so many stands
of blackjack oaks, rustling dry limbs
throughout November, holding
their leaves as long as they can.

The Work

With a finger's chipped polish, she follows
the necklace of thorns, the mattress
sprouting its exquisite
nails, Frida Kahlo's face held still
within the metal brace, that metaphoric trellis
blooming pain. My niece is quiet,
regarding this, the inward world
that art discloses, Francis Bacon's tortured corpses
untranscendent of the flesh. Later,
just inches from "The Harrowing
of Hell," she surveys the skull's
misshapen cave and hilltop where,
since 1575, the tiny writhing damned
have danced. The museum seems
negotiable, comprehensible as the urge
she sometimes feels to burn herself,
or the careful stoic carving on her arm.
Outside, the day is warm, spring
flecking its first, early contrasts
through prevailing grays and browns.
I would like to tell her
of the alpine silver lupine—how its seeds,
found frozen in a lemming's nest, stayed in stasis
through the glacial freeze, ten thousand years
before her father hurt her and we didn't know.
When excavated, planted, each seed bloomed.
I think she believes endurance
disallows ambrosial moments, adolescent bravery

stowing stones inside her heart. And yet
her eyes are still the four-year-old's
who stands in sunlit pictures
from my wedding, who now watches,
silent, from behind the jewelry of her body-piercing,
blue-black hair, her scars.
Brittle chrysalis, catharsis
is a gallery she builds around her.
When she needed us, we failed. I want
to tell her of the arctic toad that freezes solid,
thaws, and sings the summer back.
I want her to see bright sky-and-
cowskull, Georgia O'Keeffe's
cactus-rose-among-the-bones. I want—
but she is thinking, and she lets me
stand beside her while she looks.

American Dipper

Office politics
and the pettiness of each day—

the mind thickens and dries,
a whorl of driftwood.

I keep trying to picture
the American Dipper, to remember

its ordinary body plunging under
the water's surface;

the Dipper walks upstream, tiny climber
of mountains, traveller between worlds.

I stare across the long
emptiness of the desk.

The river is moving,
memory must

be breathing a specific
afternoon of alpine

light, the rapid
Rio Hondo all motion

and matter—the battered stones'
slow stumble seaward,

and the nondescript, unmistakable bird
who dives into the cold

factual current, eyes open.

Jim Bachae's New Hip

We meet him paused past fields
of glacier lily, ambling
through blue stickseed
and the day's last warm sun,
heading back the way we'd all come.
We talk briefly of things
we've seen: the eagle
perched on Haystack Butte, the wild
placid bighorn sheep, the—
what was it? marmot? badger?
wolverine? He leans against the certain
face of rock, explains he's going
slow and careful; this new hip
should last him thirty years, at least
until he's well past ninety.
Shirt worn thin at the shoulders
from the pack strap, Mr. Bachae gestures
to the cliff so close above us,
the sublime's tectonic spine.
"Do you notice," he says, delighted,
"the light on the lichen—
gold along the Garden Wall."
Below us, to the west and south,
McDonald Creek hurls
white and turquoise water west
to the penultimate Pacific surf.
River of rock dust, flowering stonecrop, we
look back to the Pleistocene's recent

leavings, the U-shaped valley curving open
like inverted ribs, a half-cupped hand,
some vast intimate curve
of body, accepting now diurnal
cloud and sudden changing light.

Parietal

I.
Two elk cross the immediate
field of sight, disappearing
into mountain forest
moss–deep green, like the dream

that sometimes finds the house:
in the side yard's grass and asters,
cougars,
        canopied antlers:
caribou with outstretched necks —

We can hear the quick
hoof-beat drum;
               they're gone.

II.
Like an animal in the mind,
the dream has left my body
startled into watchfulness, my heart
fast footsteps on the pathway back
from sleep.
           I've seen these
forms so clearly I could close
my eyes and call them back,
warm blood and charcoal,
painting themselves against
the nearby dark.

III.

Once, a boy was lost,
deep snow and flimsy
jacket, sneakers already
soaked from the hours he'd wandered
through dusk-hung woods.

In the morning, found
at last by worried searchers,
he told how two brown forms
unfolded from the forest's depths
and gently settled, warm and breathing,
right beside him through the night;
they stayed until sunlight
crested a hilltop, illuminating

just where the boy returned, midmorning,
showing where the elk had bedded down
to save a tiny, furless child.

Aesthetics and Necessity

I. SACRAMENT
The sky's gentle dusking
each evening; the familiar
emergence, through impossible distance,
of visible stars. Love,
the predictable world is
lovely, as we turn our charmed,
expectant faces outward.
How beautiful, in turn,
the ripe grasses turning to rust,
the compass plant sheathed
in frost, the redbuds coloring
the draw, and then, days later,
the thrill of leaves.

Give me your hand, I say,
and already you have.

II. SURREALISM
In darkness, the plains extend,
unseen, forever.
                    I can't imagine
mountains, forests, interrupting

this rhythm of presence, this soil.
The road ahead makes comfortable bends
as the headlights quicken toward home.

Late March, the air is chilly.

In the distance, orange light gleams
like a great city seen
from the air, minutes before landing.

Prairie fire, but I shiver, seeing
cities burning, the horizon consumed
in spectacular, terminal combustion.

III. GLEN CANYON
The fire, a freight train
of sound, would have leaped
and converged, the newscast says,
plume-dominated. Gusting flames
transformed the canyon, abandoning
the charred and standing pines,
the fine-
drawn dusting of ash,
the crumpled human dead.

In those last, furnaced moments,
could attention shift from terror
to the beloved
curve of someone's face, the cadence
of a parent's voice,
these clear perceptions
giving us ourselves?

IV. WATERSHED
Late afternoon light
dresses the grasses
in joy. King's Creek slips
along its turfy banks;
a few sedges trail green fronds

in the current. Ahead the trail
curves its sensual promise:
each quivering breath
is enough, touches me
here, yes, here.

Western Grebe in Mountain Light

Twenty hours and four thousand feet
after last night's alpine hail,
I am so tired I'm leaning
on columns of wind, on slant-light,
on this repose bordering storm.

The San Luis basin is draped
in clouds, rainfall sheeting
the valley's far end. Here, sunlight
strikes the lakes, half-washes my face
in the wind's brisk chill.

White front against
black back, the bird is
the edge of weather, breast feathers
glinting like sunlight, like ice,
the piles of hailstones that shone

by the tent in the day's last
brilliance, the mountain's
dark form above us, cloud-shrouded,
the granitic truth of extremes:
Stone, ice, water, lichen, and then

in morning's giddying descent, a dance
of plant life—late summer flowers,
the casting aspen branches, leaves quick
in the sun like water tossed
from the grebe's bright neck.

Northwest Passage

We walk across cottongrass   flox
lichen and moss where the headwaters flow
from the season's snowmelt.

We follow old glaciers   wildflowers
murdered Nez Perces.
A few large hoofprints: moose.

Beyond the marked trail we're
kneeling in eons of stone-
dust   stonecrop   pearly

everlasting   the beautiful work
of the world. Like impressionist flames rosy
paintbrush reddens the high meadow.

Explorer gentian presents
its night-blue throat   one
after another.   In this the middle

of my life I try carrying
nothing everything only
what each day I can lift in the pack.

Last night as if cobbled in light
the Milky Way showed one of the many
visible directions.

Into These Places

1. "Exploring an Unknown Region in the United States"
— ROBERT W. LIMBERT, *National Geographic* (1920)

One morning in May,
W. L. Cole and I, both of Boise,
left Minidoka, packing on our backs
bedding, an aluminum cook outfit,
a 5 × 7 camera and tripod, binoculars,
and supplies, sufficient for two weeks,
making a total pack each of 55 pounds.
We also took with us an Airedale terrier
for a camp dog. This was a mistake,
for after 3 days' travel his feet
were worn raw and bleeding.

In some places it was necessary to carry him.

Water is hidden deep in tanks or holes
at the bottom of large blowouts
and is found only by following
old Indian or mountain sheep trails
or by watching the flight of birds
as they drop into these places
to quench their thirst.
                          We were surprised
to find old bear tracks, into which the wind
had carried a species of plant seed,
pygmy buckwheat, that had taken root
and exactly filled the tracks.

Think of tracking a grizzly bear
that had crossed here possibly
hundreds of years before!
We called this place
Bear Track Flat.

Stretching to the southwest
for a distance of about 11 miles,
we saw perhaps one of the most remarkable
lava flows in the world.
Its color is a deep cobalt blue,
with generally a high gloss, as if
the flow had been given a coat
of blue varnish. The surface
is melted and veined with small cracks,
having the appearance of the scales
of some prehistoric reptile.
Mr. Israel C. Russell, at one time of the United States
Geological Survey, called it Blue Dragon Flow.

It is a place of color
and silence, the latter broken only
by the wail of the coyote
and the chirp of the rock cony.

II. CONTEXTS
Washington Irving's
rendition of Captain Bonneville's impression
reads: "Where nothing meets
the eye but a desolate and awful
waste, where no
grass grows, nor water runs,

and where nothing is
to be seen but lava."
                              Across the continent,
thinking of the world at hand,
George Inness wrote of the painter's task:
"Simply to reproduce
in other minds the impression
which a scene has made upon him
—a work of art aims
not to instruct, not to edify,
but to awaken an emotion,"
                              and in Maine, Thoreau:
"rocks, trees, wind on our cheeks!
the *solid* earth! the *actual* world!
the *common sense! Contact! Contact!*"

Decades later, at the scene,
Bob Limbert noted, "Were I gifted with the art
of word painting, I might
in some small way suggest
the wonderful coloring of these
craters. Picture yourself standing
in some vast amphitheater
whose towering walls are a riot of
yellow, green, orange, brown, and black,
with brick red and vermilion predominating.
Imagine, too, an awesome,
enveloping silence.
                    I noticed
that at places like these
we had almost nothing to say."

III. "CRATERS OF THE MOON"
A'a, pahoehoe, syllabic
archipelagoes ringed
by the broad Pacific.

Or sterility—dead, dry
lunar dust, the surface pocked
by comets, extinct meteors.

No—I think
of despair, slow
viscous fissure, rift,
self-scarring basalt
                    and below, the older
earthbones, rhyolite hard in depths
to two miles down.

The soul selects her own society—

stalactites, ice and sulfate, ooze
or bloom along the inner
flesh of caves, old lava tubes
long cooled and hollow.

Blue dragons, blue devils,
blue moon-
            light dusting
the cinder soil;

dwarf buckwheat, silver-ashen,
white tiny spires of scabland penstamon,

pale flowering bitterroot—

then shuts the door—

           like stone—

Fauve

— after Emily Carr

High northern
summer, red cedar.

A momentary inner
mist, or shiver, under-
growth and full
tree cover.
                    Boreal portal,
dark lintel, living rotting
moss depth and the vertical—

Pallor. Quiet. Shifting
light, like paint, auroral,

and a somber interior
whisper, color.

Slow Air

I. ALLEGHENY FRONT

Geosyncline

Sunlight and sediment,
slabs of the planet gather
under coastal water.

The Paleozoic ocean opens,
closes, opens, such a slow
aortal pulse.
                    No one
to abstract, no one to quantify,

while mountains ripple
their accreted height,
Appalachian, Caledonian,

four thousand miles of sutured earth.

Peat Bog

Mist drifts in from the distant
hillside.
                    Red cedars' ragged branches
disappear for minutes, seconds,
slow gestures motionless
between the thickest folds
of fog.

It shifts—
mist quickens, disappears.

In sunlight, warming sphagnum moss
grows pungent. Sundews wait,
their spined leaves open
in archaic hunger.

Light strikes the cottongrass,
tiny white sedges lifting
from the trembling earth.

The bog exhales its stagnant bloom.

II. CONVERSATION

*. . . we start from the old phrase "he was on hunting," which
meant "he was in the course of hunting, engaged in hunting, busy
with hunting"; he was, as it were, in the middle of something,
some protracted action or state, denoted by the substantive "hunt-
ing." Here "on" became phonetically "a," as in other cases, and
"a" was eventually dropped, exactly as in other phrases: "burst out
on laughing, a-laughing, laughing; fall on thinking, a-thinking,
thinking . . ."*

going,
    a-going,
        ongoing

*Table 18 also presents clear-cut support for the contention that "a-
prefixing" is dying out in Appalachia. The eight speakers with the
highest relative frequency levels for "a-prefixing" are all age 50 or
older. Only three of the 13 speakers represented in the table are
under age 30, and these three speakers all reveal "a-prefixing" at
levels under 20 percent.*

In third grade Russell Cullems
brought ginseng to school, *ginsang,*
'sang, said after recess he was making
ginsang tea. We tasted some in paper cups
before the teacher knew. Russell said
they gathered ginseng in the hills to sell.
After sixth grade, Russell's family
moved away. I can't remember if I ever
knew just where they went,
and it was close to thirty years ago.

Singe, singest, singe, singe, singest, singeth, singen,

singin'
          ongoing

The formation of verb past tenses in English has evolved from a
more complex system of inflectional endings (including at one
point, for example, a distinction between singular and plural in the
preterit, which survives today only in the "was" and "were" forms
of "to be").

I was, you was, they was—

                              —But it was years ago.

III. FIDDLE-
          head ferns, from a forest
of ferns, knee-high, thigh-
high, feathering the scattered
granite under yellow birch
and rhododendron.

An interval of sun
descends through tree leaves,
gleams briefly
vivid green.

Pinch off the top,
the fern's curl like
the fiddle's scroll,
steam till tender, toss
with bacon grease, or butter.
Mix oatmeal, barley, shortening, salt,
bake over the open fire, turning
once to brown—
bannock bread, journey cake.

And after supper listen
to the wind, mountain
music, Celtic fiddle,
miner
          crofter,
all the songs
of loss and distance.

Slow air, a music carrying
the single flower
by the broken step,
the window open to the evening prospect,
guitar or fiddle lifting
with a woman's voice, continuing
when she falls silent.

The Blue of the Mussel Shell

—after Andrew Wyeth

Sight lingers along
the near angle of weathered
lumber.
      What anchors
our attention, what
endures?
      Indoors,
geraniums redden the distance
the eye must move, from the blue
shoulder where a woman
sits working, to the ringed
blue stasis of a mason
jar, and the possible
ocean, blue beyond
the windowpane.

Light lifts into
the sky's finite horizons,
which are also vast.

Or the sea darkens, the blue
door closes, the mind
crosses the horizontal
whale bone beached
in the loose litter
of edges, settles
where the blue of the mussel shell
colors this prospect, giving, just now,
the last light back.